T0043555

ANGEL NUMBERS

AN ENCHANTING MEDITATION BOOK OF SPIRIT GUIDES AND MAGIC

Fortuna Noir

wellfleet
press

Introduction

From the dawn of humankind, we as a species have felt
a connection to our planet, the Universe, and the Divine.
Throughout history, humans have worshipped the Sun, the
Moon, the four elements—earth, air, fire, and water—and, of
course, the deities that span the physical and the abstract
characteristics of life: love, war, peace. It's practically in our
nature to look toward forces larger and more powerful than
we are. As a result of our search, religions like Hinduism,
Judaism, and Buddhism were born and are still practiced to
this day. We cannot resist the call to our spiritual sides no
matter how hard we try, even as some try much harder than
others. We are not solely physical beings. We are spiritual
beings in physical bodies; what truly nourishes our souls is
our connection to the supernatural.

Because the gods don't speak to us directly, we have found several practices to connect to the Divine, such as sacrifices, magic spells, complex rituals, praying, and numerology. In one iteration, numerology is the study of the numerical values in words and letters. This practice dates back to the eighth century. Arabian, Chinese, and Indian cultures have used numerology as a way to assign numbers to letters in their respective alphabets. Here, people are given soul numbers based on their birth names or the date they were born. Within this same school of thought, numerology is the belief that numbers have energies that coincide with certain traits. For example, the number 2 is considered feminine. Someone whose soul number is 2 might be characterized as supportive or influential.

In this book, we will talk about angel numbers, a subsect of numerology. Instead of assigning numbers to people, angel numbers are all about interpreting the messages behind the numbers that appear in our lives. In this belief system, angels communicate with us by sending us individual numbers or a sequence of numbers to first, get our attention, and second, to send a message from God to us. You might be asking yourself why they use numbers instead of speaking to us directly. The answer is that numbers are everywhere. They are one of the first things we learn in school and we tend to notice when we're seeing repeat numbers. After you become familiar with their meanings, you will see that numbers can be just as effective as words.

Another tenet in angel numbers is the belief that "God" refers to the Creator of the Universe, not a being instilled in human religions. The Creator is a being of infinite love, watching over us and respecting our free will enough to send us helpful messages to try to steer us in the right direction. When you receive messages from the angels and you want clarification, feel free to ask God for any extra information. God and the angels work in tandem to give you the guidance you need.

As you read on and learn more, let this book be a starting point for your spiritual journey. But also, be open to any additional insight from your angels or anything you intuitively interpret.

One important aspect of reading angel numbers is paying attention to when they come to you and what you feel when you see them. These will be lenses through which you read the messages more clearly. There are quite a few methods to interpret the angel numbers: combining them, reading the root numbers, paying attention to your thoughts and feelings, and asking God for discernment.

Throughout Part 1 and at the end of each angel number, you will find short meditations. Each one is meant to put you in a space to fully grasp the meaning of the section you've just read and to sit in stillness with it. Meditation is an exceptional way to clear the mind, focus on a singular concept, and let it sink in. Angel numbers have many different meanings that can be difficult to remember, so please use the meditations to embody those meanings and use them to move forward on your spiritual path.

Now is the time to begin your understanding of angels, their messages, and what they mean to you.

SO MOTE IT BE.*

* The term "So mote it be" used within is a ritual phrase historically used by Freemasons, and currently used by Neopagan practitioners translated to mean "So it must be."

1

Angels

NGELS ARE UBIQUITOUS beings throughout human history. Their iconography can be found on chapel ceilings, in Renaissance paintings, in cartoons as winged beings on our shoulders, and in video games as beautiful, ethereal creatures. They're considered symbols of pure righteousness, ruled by an obligation to always do the right thing on behalf of God. They're so much a part of our lives that they're woven into our lexicon. If someone calls you an angel, it means they think you're sweet and innocent. If you call someone your angel, it's like saying they're your guardian who watches over you.

Yet, despite how we view angels, many of us don't take a moment to understand what angels are or what part they play in the Universe. The reason for this might be that in many religions, God is the sole focus of attention. Angels are secondary to God and they do what is asked of them. In this chapter, you will learn what angels are, how they communicate with us, and what role they play in our lives. Once you're done, you will be ready to begin your relationship with these divine creatures and be primed to read the numbers they send your way.

What Are Angels?

The word "angel" comes from the Greek word *anglos*, which means "messenger" or "heralder." This means that angels are heavenly messengers of God. They are spiritual beings who do not abide by our rules or logic. Instead, they are eternal entities who are meant to spread God's love to us, protect us, and empower us to achieve our life purpose.

They do not follow our conventions, but instead operate on their own frequencies and energies for the greater good of humanity. They move on God's behalf, never acting on their own. Rather, they are an extension of God, so whenever you encounter one, know it is because the Creator has sent them to you.

As physical beings, we tend to think of divine agents in our own image. You cannot do this with angels. Because they are spirits, they do not have a body as we understand one to be. We may perceive them as bursts of light, elusive beings in our peripheral vision, or simply a presence we cannot explain. It is more accurate to think of them as ethereal essences who have our best intentions at heart and want to tell and show us what we can do to be more holistic humans with high-vibrational energies.

Why Do Angels Exist?

Angels exist to serve God and humanity as God sees fit. In Christianity, the main task is in their name: Angels are to be messengers. Famously, angels have bestowed good news to humans—like the birth of Jesus—but also premonitions like the entire Book of Revelations. In the same faith, it's believed that angels are warriors of God, battling with their fallen counterparts to block their evil influence on the world. Angels are also meant to be guardians of humans. According to the Bible, they can release prisoners and protect people from harm when all seems lost. They are very capable entities.

In Yazdânism, also known as the Cult of Angels, one of its founding principles is the idea that God has put seven divine beings in charge of the world. These seven beings, made of pure light, defend the earth from malevolent forces. Within the seven divine beings is the chief archangel, Melek Taus, who goes by his other title, the Peacock Angel. According to Yazdânism, Melek Taus is somewhat of an untouchable entity who is able to bestow benevolence, responsibilities, and malevolence at his own discretion, making him more like God than any other angel.

In Islam, angels have various roles, such as guarding Paradise and Hell, sending rain and prosperity to humans, assisting the souls of the dead to Allah, and recording a person's every action and thought throughout their lives. They are meant to assist Allah in everything. This book will primarily address the messenger angels and what they have to say to us.

What Types of Angels Are There?

According to the Catholic Church, and some works of literature not only are there different types of angels, but there's also a divine order to those angels. The first group is called the First Sphere because they live on that level of Heaven. This group is composed of three angel types: seraphim, cherubim, and thrones. Seraphim are the angels closest to God. They take care of God's throne. Cherubim are multifaced creatures with the faces of an ox, a man, a lion, and an eagle. Like the angels we normally picture, they have wings, though theirs have eyes all over them. They guard the road to the Tree of Life. The thrones, like their namesake, literally carry God's throne, but they also carry messages from God to the lower-level angels.

The next grouping is called the Second Sphere. The angels that make up this group are *dominions*, *virtues*, and *powers*. Dominions manage the duties of the lower angels. They are carriers of justice but they also value love and peace. Virtues are very special. They have a profound power to bring miracles and signs to the world. When people say they feel as though an angel has intervened in their lives, they're more than likely referring to virtues. Powers are the warrior angels. They fight against evil like soldiers in God's army, fully decked out in armor.

Last, there is the Third Sphere. These angels are the principalities, archangels, and angels. Principalities are the third closest to Earth, and by proxy, us humans. They assist the higher angels in whatever duties are needed. They are guardians of the earth itself. Next are the archangels. They look over each nation and, at times, appear to humans to deliver a message. Some well-known archangels are Michael and Gabriel. The lowest angels, and the ones closest to humans, are the angels. These are the beings we most often color as human-looking figures with flowing robes and big, wide wings. These angels are most likely to carry God's messages to us, especially in the form of numbers.

How Involved Are Angels in Our Lives?

How involved angels are in our lives depends on the type of angel. The angels in the Third Sphere are the closest to us, which means we are one of their main concerns. Though they protect us and send us messages, they do not directly intervene in anything we do. We have free will and that means we have full control of ourselves. The downside is we may not always know when we are on the right path if we don't take the time to look at the signs around us.

The angels' primary goal is to mind us and guide us on our life path as much as we allow them to. Because we have power over our lives, we can also choose to ignore or simply not pay attention to what the angels or God have to say to us. This does not mean they're not around us. Instead, it means it is our choice to take advantage of what they want to show us or continue on without their wisdom.

In this life, no matter what, we are never alone. They are cheering us on because they carry the same love that God has for us. Take a moment to call for them.

- Sit in a comfortable position with your back straight.

- Play meditative music to clear your mind.

- Take two deep breaths to lower your brain waves and raise your vibrations.

Meditation

Close your eyes and picture yourself alone in space.
You are safe here, closest to the angels.
Open your mind's eye and imagine yourself
covered in a glow, like a beacon.
This will attract the angels to you.
Then ask God to send them your way.
Sit still and wait for them to show themselves to you
as bodiless but beautiful beings.
When they arrive, ask them to send you numbers often.
Promise them you will look for them.
Thank them and let them embrace you.

How Do We Communicate with Angels?

We as humans do not communicate directly with angels. Rather, we speak to God and God gives the messages to them. But that does not mean we shouldn't try to do our part to make communication easier. Instead of trying to figure out what we can do to speak to the angels, we should instead focus on what we can do so they can more readily speak to *us*.

To begin, we must take a look at our vibrations. Everything that exists is made of vibrating matter, including us. These vibrations determine whether an object is soft, hard, solid, or gaseous. Angels operate at a much higher frequency than we do because they are not made of matter, so much so that they must lower their vibrations to speak to us.

In order to better hear their messages, we have to raise our vibrational energies to meet them. This can be done in several ways. One way is to get healthy, meaning eating right, exercising, and taking care of our physical bodies so that we feel good overall. Positive emotions bring about higher energies.

The second way is to improve our emotional state. If you tend to stress out, remind yourself that if you can breathe deeply, you are safe at the current moment. If you have been feeling down, do what makes you happy. Tending to your emotional and mental health will open you up to receiving all that the angels have to offer you.

And the third avenue is to enhance our spiritual side. Because we live in a physical world, we tend to focus on the physical: our jobs, homes, relationships, etc. As a result, it's so easy to forget that you are a spiritual being in a physical body. Your spirit needs tending to as well. To do this you can meditate, speak to God directly, or perform rituals. All these actions are ways to raise your energies so you can meet the angels where they are and hear their messages more clearly. Let's take a moment to do just that.

♦ Sit in a comfortable position.

♦ Take two deep breaths to clear your mind.

♦ Play emotionally uplifting music.

*In your mind's eye, picture a source of light
with no defining characteristics.
This is what an angel looks like. Think of them as energies.
Now reach into yourself and take hold of your energy.
Concentrate on it and imagine yourself vibrating with power.
Let it flow from your core into your limbs,
your hands and feet, and your third eye.
Become a being made of energy.*

Use this meditation whenever you need to raise your vibrations to meet the angels.

How Do Angels Communicate with Us?

Because angels are not physical beings, they cannot speak
to us as we can speak to each other. They do not have
the throats we have and thereby cannot talk like we can.
However, there are a few ways they communicate with us.
The first is our thoughts and feelings, but this can be best
interpreted when we are open to receiving their messages.
In general, we are not taught to listen to our feelings. We
experience them, react to them, and get over them. But with
angels, it is important to pay attention to what they might
be trying to tell you. If you get a feeling, like a tug on your
intuition, this could be a sign the angels are trying to speak to
you. This is something you will have to learn to look out for.

With how busy we are, it can be difficult to slow down and listen to what we are feeling or experiencing, and even harder to see the signs that might be right in front of us. Thankfully, this is surmountable because angels use our thoughts and feelings *and* numbers to speak to us, so we have multiple avenues to be aware of.

If feeling and thinking are the conduits, numbers are the messages themselves. This can be literally any number, as long as it stands out to you. If you see a sequence of numbers and you feel as though they are special somehow, chances are you're looking at angel numbers. They need to mean something to you in order for them to be important. From there you can go about deciphering what the angels are trying to tell you. We will go into what the numbers mean in Chapter 2.

Next, we will see what types of messages angels send us.

General Messages

Overall, angels communicate via three types of messages: general messages, specific messages, and advanced messages. General messages are exactly as they sound—they are not specific to one person. They can apply to virtually anybody. It is best to think of them as universal truths that anyone can stop, read, and get something from. Typically, they range from the numbers 0 to 9 because those are the root numbers. They are the foundation of angel numbers as a whole.

Receiving a general message is similar to seeing an inspirational poster. They are everywhere and they contain a good message, but not everyone stops to notice them. However, if you notice them, you were meant to notice. You were meant to get something out of it, and if you take the time to accept what you see, then you will.

General messages are typically supposed to guide you. They exist to let you know whether you are on the right path or whether you need to make a change or two. They are gentle markers of where you stand and how you can get to the next step successfully. Angels also use them as reminders that you are loved and you are being watched over. So, take what they have to say as advice and use it to inspire you. Later, you will learn what each number means and how to apply it to your life.

Specific Messages

Specific messages take one step further than general messages because they are typically a response to whatever it is you were just thinking or feeling. They are specific to you and your situation. For example, if you have been feeling lost in life, like you're adrift on a raft going nowhere, you may see the number 6, which means you need to find stability and balance. If you see 6 every time you feel lost or confused, then you have your specific message. It is a guiding light from the angels, who are trying to give you the solution to your problem. Specific messages are like directional signs telling you which way you need to go so that you can keep moving forward and get back on the right spiritual and emotional path.

The best part about these messages is that they are a clear indicator that the angels not only see you but hear you as well. Angels are able to sense our vibrations and energies. Because of this, if you see an angel number that perfectly matches you at that moment, know that they are reaching out to *you*. And because they're reaching out to you, you can rest assured that they understand you. When you need a sign, it can feel as though no one truly understands what you are going through. But this is not the case. You are seen and you are loved.

In order to see these signs, you have to learn to pay attention. When we are consumed with our feelings and cannot see what is around us, that is when we are stuck. We might wallow in sadness or confusion and not see a way out. During these troubling times, you have to make an effort to listen and look to see what message God has for you. Next, you will have to get even more familiar with what the numbers mean so that you will have an easier time knowing what the angels are trying to say.

Advanced Messages

Advanced messages come when you are further along on your spiritual journey. Once you've learned to read the numbers and become familiar with their energies, you will be better able to decode the more complex messages. By the time you begin to receive these messages, you will have had to raise your vibrations as you become closer to the angels. And this means you will be more receptive.

When the angels are trying to send you advanced numbers, you will see several repeated angel number sequences in a row. For example, you might wake up in the middle of the night to see the clock read 4:44 a.m. Then, if you watch TV, you might see a commercial advertising a product that costs $9.99 and so on. When you receive these messages, the angels are trying to get your attention.

33 1111 999 7

At this point, the energies of the numbers themselves don't matter as much as what you are experiencing when you receive the numbers. Let's say you are caught between two decisions and you need to make a choice soon. You may begin to see 111 or 222 a lot. When this happens, you must pay attention to what you were feeling before you saw the numbers and what you felt during. With those two things in mind, you can then decipher what the angels are trying to tell you. Advanced messages are always calls to action and they are specific to you and what is currently happening in your life. Combining all these aspects will help you determine whether your angels want to guide you to a different point of view or whether they want you to charge forward with renewed passion.

What Do Angels Want for Us?

The one thing the angels want from us is to heed their advice and guidance. Every number they send our way always carries a positive message no matter which one is sent. It might be a number of encouragement, like a 3 or a 7, or a warning like the number 9. No matter the number, it is always delivered with love. Because of this, it is important to keep the lines of communication open with them. Angels can influence your thoughts and feelings, which means they want to fill you with positivity and light. They have been around for millennia, so they know how difficult life can be for humans.

They know we live on a plane of existence that can be hostile to our well-being. They see that the societies we live in can repress or even crush us at times. They understand that we need help to move forward in this life we've been given.

They also want us to meet our fullest potential. Don't mistake this as they want us to be perfect because nothing in the material world is perfect. Instead, they want to see us win and thrive. When we are aware of who we are, where we are, what we are, and how we move about in the world around us, we are living our most authentic selves. It is a place of constant growth and progression. Though this does not mean we will *always* progress as we would like to, it does mean we are moving forward. The angels simply want what is best for us, no matter what that looks like. And so, they are here to steer us in the right direction as much as they are able, and as much as we let them.

♦ Sit in a comfortable position with your hands open, ready to receive.

♦ Put on calming music.

Meditation

Think about what you want out of your connection
with the angels and what they want for you.
It's a symbiotic relationship that begins with you.
Open your arms as well as your hands and say aloud:
"Dear God, thank you for the angels.
Today is the day I openly embrace them
and what they have to show and tell me.
I will accept their messages and better myself
to fulfill my life purpose."
Lift your hands, raise your energy,
and feel God's love pouring into you.
You're beginning to become in tune with the Divine.

What Do We Gain by Listening to Angels?

We have *everything* to gain by listening to the angels. There are lessons to learn, life-molding experiences to be had, self-love to discover, and synchronicity with God and the supernatural world that lies just beyond what we can see and touch.

We don't necessarily *need* to commune with angels to live fulfilling lives. There are many people who don't believe in their existence and seemingly manage just fine. But anyone can simply get by, that is what the majority of life is—forging ahead because that is simply how time works. However, the quality of your life and experiences can be drastically different without any assistance or counsel. If there's a sign that says DEAD END and you decide to ignore it, you will find yourself stuck at the end of the road. But if you acknowledge it and make the choice to move away from it, you will have saved yourself some time as well as some unnecessary trouble. The same is true for these heavenly spirits. Their guidance can help you move about in a clearer, more direct way so that you can avoid feeling lost and unsure.

With their help, you can focus what little time you have on this planet and use it in a way that honors you. You have a purpose on this earth, and though the angels won't directly tell you what it is, they can lead you to it, so you can discover it yourself. You never *need* to follow anyone or anything, but imagine what you might miss out on!

You might also lose out on being embraced by God's love in a way that feels personal to you. God loves all creations, and wants you to feel the love They have for you. The angels are one of the conduits to God's love. If you keep your spiritual vibrations high, you will be able to feel so much more than if you don't. Love and compassion are what guide these angels to you. Take what they have to offer.

How Do We Foster a Relationship with Angels?

The best way to cultivate a relationship with angels is to listen to what they are trying to tell you because whatever message they have for you is in your favor. If you have a friend who asks you for advice, but they never listen to what you have to say, your relationship will suffer. You're only trying to help, but they don't seem to care. This plays out similarly to your relationship with angels. If you ignore them long enough, they won't show themselves to you anymore. So, to feel their affection for you, you must foster a level of awareness.

Consider them as your teachers or guardians watching over you. Even though they are around you, it is important to remember that they are an extension of God. So, if you want a relationship with them, you also want to have a good relationship with God. You can do this by praying and thanking God for what They are doing in your life and what They have shown you. You can also ask for help whenever you need it. This is important because so many of us tend to close up when we want help instead of asking for what we need. Admitting you need assistance is a form of vulnerability, and being vulnerable is where true relationships can grow. Be open to what the angels have to say, accept the love they are trying to give you, and want better for yourself in the process.

What Can We Do
for Angels?

Angels are not creatures like us who need regular validation and assurances. Thereby, they don't need anything from us. They have their place in the divine order where they fulfill the roles God has for them. If you want to please them, the best thing you can do is to live an in-tune life, and that means taking care of yourself emotionally, mentally, and spiritually. Be aware of your feelings and thoughts and how they affect you. Try to stay away from destructive patterns like brutal self-talk, being unforgiving of yourself, taking your frustrations out on others, or refusing to accept the help you need.

If you are open, no matter how well your life is going, they will communicate with you, but they can show you so much more if you are in a more relaxed state.

- ♦ Sit in a comfortable position.
- ♦ Make sure you're well fed and calm.

Meditation

As you sit in stillness, take a moment
to recognize that you are full.
There isn't anything you need to worry about.
Keep your mind free and be open
to whatever feelings or thoughts come to you.
After the feelings have come and gone,
make this promise to yourself aloud:
"As I strive to listen to the angels,
I will take care of myself along the way.
I am important and I will ensure my cup is full
before pouring it into anyone else.
I will better myself not only for the angels,
but for me as well.
I will be true to myself."

2

Root Numbers

ROOT NUMBERS REFER TO THE numbers 0 to 9 and, in this case, 10. They are the building blocks of both angel numbers and numerology. When read in order, they can represent the beginning of life, which starts at 0, to the end of a cycle that may end at 9 and can restart at 10. Or they can be read as markers of your progress during your spiritual path. This is why it is imperative to listen to your thoughts and feelings when you receive these messages. They will be responses to what is going on in your life, a warning of what is to come, or a sign of encouragement.

In this chapter, you will learn the importance and characteristics of each number and what their presence means in your life. While exploring each number's energies and messages, you will become intimately familiar with their meanings. Once you have these messages down, you will be able to learn how to read more complex number combinations. But for now, get to know each number and discover how they can apply to your life circumstances or your truest emotions and dreams. This is the first step to connecting with your angels and seeing what they have in store for you and your journey.

Angel Number

0

The number 0 is one of the most powerful numbers in existence. When in its natural form, 0 is a complete and perfect circle, representing eternity. There is no beginning or end, only infinity. Because of this, 0 simultaneously holds energy and lets it pass through. It is feminine in its nature, meaning it is about balance and receptivity.

When you keep seeing 0, it means you are at the beginning of a spiritual journey, filled with unknowns. It is a number of infinite possibilities, much like the start of something new. It holds all potentialities and outcomes in its shape and energy, meaning you face those same destinies. When you see 0, it means the angels are showing you a sign of what is to come, that you are about to embark on a new path. It is an exciting time of adventure and exploration.

Though it may seem frightening, 0 is actually meant to be comforting. If you are stuck in an unwanted situation, 0 can be the hope that change is coming. With angel numbers, any sign is a good sign. Do not be afraid. Instead, embrace what God and the angels have in store for you.

As its shape implies, 0 is also a circle similar to being encircled in an embrace, or part of a community. If you are seeing 0, it could also mean you are being surrounded by love and light. God and the angels are trying to tell you that you are not alone. Instead, you are surrounded by those who wish to love and protect you. It is the energy of communion and will aid you on your new spiritual journey. You have the supernatural on your side.

Because of its power to multiply other numbers, 0 is also a sign of augmentation. What was once 1 is now 10, magnifying the 1's energy. What is 10 can become 100, further intensifying its power. Immense strength may come from 0, so if you are seeing this number, it means you have the ability to create and enhance the situations in your life. You have a choice, even if you do not always believe you do. You are equipped with your own inner strength and that of the Divine.

- ◆ Sit comfortably in a quiet location.

- ◆ Play soothing music or insert earplugs to help you concentrate.

- ◆ Hold a circular object, like a ring, in your hand to represent 0.

Meditation

Hold the object in your hand and trace its shape.
Imagine the object sparking as if being lit on fire.
This is the power of 0.
Now, imagine a circular door in front of you.
This door represents your future.
Take the power of 0 and walk toward the door,
knowing you have all the potential you need.
Open it and feel the light on the other side envelop you.
Your new life has begun.

Angel Number

1

The number 1 is a mighty and sacred number. It encompasses so many aspects of the Universe, similar to 0, but is concentrated into one entity. The number 1 represents all that is. We are connected to the Divine, the Universe, and everything that exists. So if you see this number often, the angels are sending you a reminder that you are a spiritual being who is integrated into the world around you. Synchronicity with the Divine is part of what propels us forward. It reminds us that we are capable of great things because we are living in our truth and have the support of our angels.

The number 1 has many interpretations to it. If you're seeing 1 frequently, one of the messages might be an indication of a new beginning. Everything starts with 1—the first step on an adventure, the first breath a baby takes, and the first step of a plan. So, if you see 1, it might indicate that you are about to embark on a new venture. Perhaps you have wanted to start a hobby, a career, or a friendship, but for whatever reason, you have not taken the steps to do so. With 1, the angels are telling you that they support you on your unprecedented adventure.

Because 1 is the number of beginnings, it can indicate that change is coming soon. A time of manifestation might be upon you. Whether you have a dream you would like to see actualized or a goal you'd like to reach, it's of the utmost importance to stay positive. There is power in our thoughts, and they can shape our future by influencing our actions for better or for worse. Think about what life will be like when your aspirations come true. Stick with those thoughts and avoid negative thinking as much as you can.

Number 1 is also about risks. As people, it is in our nature to want to stick with a routine. Routines are safe and worry-free. We know what's going to happen in our day, so there will be no surprises, which we equate to being safe. But constantly hiding behind "safety" means we miss out on opportunities for growth or something life changing. When you see 1 and you have been stuck in a rut, take this as a sign to open your awareness to new opportunities.

♦ Sit in a comfortable position.

♦ Hold a single object that gives you power.

Meditation

Close your eyes and imagine yourself pulling
strength from the object into yourself.
Use the object as an anchor to the physical world.
Now envision the angels making a circle tightly around you.
Feel the warmth radiating from them to you.
Together you become a pillar of light so bright that
it shines outside your space and into the heavens.
Revel in this light, this power, and know with the
number 1, you can do anything.

Angel Number

2

The number 2 is another sacred number that holds many attributes, but it is predominantly relational—with other people, with the angels, with God, and with yourself. On its own, 2 carries the energy of balance and harmony, as well as equity and love. It is a powerful and compelling number. When you see 2 frequently, know that it is a sign to focus not only on yourself but also on another facet of your relationship with what's around you. The number 2 might appear when you feel isolated from the people in your life and want a change. Follow its warning and get integrated into your community.

This number is also about service and compassion. In North American societies, a strong sense of individualism permeates all aspects of life. Because of this, it is easy to become fixated on ourselves and what we are going through and not enough on how we can help others. Perhaps you know someone who is struggling financially. Instead of showing sympathy, you could take your actions a step further and ask what you can do for them. It is about showing compassion and actively helping those who need it. And as you do this, others will flock to you when you need grace.

There are moments in our lives when we are pushing ahead with what we believe are the right decisions. But sometimes doubt sneaks in and suddenly we aren't sure whether we are doing the right thing. Perhaps you received an angel number telling you to stay on a certain path, you followed it, but haven't gotten any confirmation from God that you are going in the right direction. The number 2 tells you to have faith in what is happening in your life. Maybe you have been praying for direction but haven't received an answer yet.

When you see 2, know this is the angels telling you to believe that you are going the correct way and that your prayers will be answered soon.

In order to bring about balance, we have to look at what's inside ourselves. The number 2 is a reminder that we are dual creatures. We have light and dark sides to ourselves. Everyone experiences this, and there's no shame in it. In fact, embracing the duality in us is one of the best ways to become a fuller, more loving human being. Never shy away from your dark side.

- ♦ Sit in a comfortable position.
- ♦ Hold two coins between your fingers so you can feel the differences on each side.

Meditation

Close your eyes and move your fingers along the coins' surfaces.
Think of the coins as the essence of 2.
Both have two sides, two different pictures, and two aspects
to themselves that combine to make singular objects.
Now see the coins for what they are:
ways to enrich someone else.
A coin may be a small step, but combined,
they form a force to be reckoned with.
Every good act begins with a small step that will create
a stronger force when carried out over time.
This is the nature of 2: commitment, faith, and compassion.
Know this and take it with you.

Angel Number

3

If you see the number 3 appear repeatedly, it's time to rejoice because 3 carries so many positive meanings. The first is that your prayers are being heard and they will be answered soon. Similar to 2, the number 3 is about manifestation. Unlike 2, when you encounter 3, it means your dreams have left your hands, so to speak, and now the angels and God are working to make it happen. During this time, take a moment to thank God for what They're doing in your life and be patient. When you know something good is coming your way, it can be easy to want it *now*. But you cannot rush God, so just rest knowing They have things under control.

Another interpretation of number 3 is that you are on the right spiritual path. You have done the work and tended to your spiritual side so much that you are in tune with the supernatural realm. When you are in this place, it means you have the capacity to receive more messages from the angels.

This sign is one of reassurance. The angels are trying to tell you that you are on the correct frequency. You aren't letting anything come between you and your metaphysical self, meaning you are actively nourishing your soul. Keep it up.

All humans are creative in one way or another, even if it doesn't seem like it. We are capable of building houses, creating code, and writing novels. If you are seeing 3 wherever you go, this is the angels trying to tell you to get creative. If you have a project you are currently working on, the angels want you to show the world. Though this can be intimidating, you will add to the plethora of knowledge that helps so many people. After all, not everyone creates the same way. Your specific voice can be just what the world needs.

The number 3 is an especially wonderful number because it signifies that Ascended Masters are helping you manifest your desires. An Ascended Master is someone who has risen past the physical world to intense enlightenment. Some of these masters include Jesus and Buddha. Their presence brings peace and love to you. They help you find stillness in yourself and see others through the eyes of God, thereby fostering more compassion and understanding in you. Listen closely to their lessons so you may become an even more remarkable person.

- ♦ Sit in a comfortable position.
- ♦ Take three deep breaths to raise your vibration.

Meditation

Imagine yourself walking down a hallway toward an open door.
You can't fully see what's on the other side, but you don't worry
about that because you have faith in the angels and yourself.
As you walk, hear the angels whisper in your ear,
"Keep going. You're doing great."
Then, when you step out the door, imagine your dreams manifested.
You get exactly what you wanted.
Rejoice in this and hold on to the hope it will come true.

Angel Number

4

The number 4 carries the energy of organization and base work. This number's energy comes from the stability of the earth. There are the four directions: north, east, south, and west. And there are the four elements: earth, air, fire, and water. These aspects are the bedrock of the world. Without them, we would not have the earth we know and love. So, it is important to have a good foundation so that we can truly accomplish our dreams. When 4 appears, it means we have to reevaluate our life and see what we are basing it on. Are you living with a big secret? Are you functioning off old principles that do not work for you anymore? Number 4 carries the message to refocus and adjust to what is right for you.

Working off this point, the number 4 reminds us to take care of our bodies and our physical space. If our bodies are not functioning the way they need to, life can be upended. If we live in a cluttered environment, it can make us feel frantic and out of control. When you see 4, the angels may be telling you to take care of yourself. Eat well and on time, exercise, and do activities that make you feel alive. If you've had passing thoughts that you need to clean up your space, 4 is telling you to do it for your own well-being.

Trying to become a better person comes with the cost of hard work and sacrifice. If you aren't pushing yourself to do more than you are comfortable with, you will stay stagnant. If you aren't moving, you aren't growing. When you see 4, take this as a suggestion to challenge yourself to do more. Make yourself work so that you can reap the benefits. There's nothing like getting over a difficult obstacle only to be rewarded afterward. The angels want you to experience this for yourself, so go for it.

Because the number 4 also has the energy of organization, its presence is indicative of archangels—the angels that watch over each country. If they present themselves to you, it's because they want you to know they're willing to help you on your path to achieving your dreams and goals. They want to lend themselves to you so you can continue on with your life purpose with their guidance, affection, and aid.

♦ Sit in a comfortable position with your hands folded in prayer.

Meditation

Close your eyes and let your mind go blank.

Next, picture four pillars around you.

Each pillar stands for the directions, the elements, and the angels.

Take note of every pillar and see how they hold up the roof above you.

Now picture the number 4 in front of you.

It radiates stability and power.

Say in your head, "I accept this message and I desire its ethos."

Let the energy from 4 cover you in light.

Let it stimulate your mind to change, to plan, and to work.

This will aid you in your waking life.

Take these principles and don't let them go.

Angel Number

5

The number 5 is a complex number that focuses primarily on spiritual development. It encourages us to take our past struggles and learn from them. We are made up of choices and experiences. With those, we are molded into the people we are today. Of course, not all of those experiences are positive, so we have a tendency to get stuck in the past. This number's energy says to let go of what has happened yesterday or many years ago that is still affecting you today. Not to forget, but to let it go so that you can live in the present moment.

When you begin to see 5 everywhere you turn, it is a warning that life-altering changes are coming. What occurred in your past has culminated now to influence your present. Each step you've taken has led to this moment in time. Know that when you see 5, the angels are telling you that *big* changes are coming, not small changes here and there. So be on the lookout for something major to come along and reposition your life.

Remember that the change will be a positive, so don't worry about the unknown details. Instead, focus on having an attitude of gratitude. This will help you cope better with the new alterations. The angels know that change is difficult for humans, especially unpredictable shifts in our lives. So try not to worry and instead stay in the present moment and take each new step as it comes. Pray to God and ask for peace and patience so that you can better adapt to real life. The angels will be near you to help you cope. Know that you are never alone. Have the courage to know everything will work out as it should and you will become the person you are meant to be at the end of all this.

Because of the uncertainty, it is completely normal and expected that we may panic and have moments of doubt or disbelief. When we do not know what to prepare for, it's easy to become consumed with the details and myriad questions, such as "What if I mess up?" or "What if I don't handle things well enough?" If you are experiencing this, take a moment to be kind to yourself. You are human and can only handle so much. Tell yourself no matter what happens, you will overcome it. You always do.

♦ Sit in a comfortable position.

♦ With a skin-safe marker, write the number 5 on one of your palms.

Meditation

*Look closely at the number on your hand, at the shape of it.
The bottom of 5 is a semicircle that is meant to
catch the energy that comes toward it.
In this way, you are like 5.
With the new alterations to your life, you're taking what
God has for you and carrying it with you to the next step.
With this 5 written on your hand, know that
you are the change you will receive.
Remember that change is good and you will
gracefully incorporate it into your life.
Just wait.*

Angel Number

6

As physical beings, we focus on what we can see, touch, hear, taste, and smell. Because of the society we live in, much of that is material possessions, like having nice houses, fancy cars, the latest gadgets, and other things you can buy. Having new, shiny things definitely can perk anybody up. It's nice to have an abundance of stuff around us, so we work hard to be able to buy more and more. However, it's best not to get too caught up in physical trinkets. They can get stolen, lost, or destroyed, and you will have nothing to show for it. When you see 6, it could be a sign your angels want you to slow down and put your attention on what matters.

The number 6 resonates with some of our deepest emotions. When seen, it can be a reminder to follow our hearts and evaluate the true treasures of life. For example, helping others in your personal circle and even beyond can be a wonderful calibration away from the egotistical self into a more empathetic person. Perhaps you have some skills that are unique to you that someone else needs. Seeing 6 might mean your angels are encouraging you to help someone in the way only you can.

Some of our deepest emotions reside in our strongest bonds: family. Familial relationships make up who we are as people. We are strongly influenced the most by those who raised us and who surrounded us in our formative years, even into adulthood. Family can mean different things to different people, but if you consider someone your family, it's because they have a strong bond with you. If the angels are sending you a 6, it could mean you need to stray from material obsession and come back to your roots and the people who love you unconditionally. These relationships are what life is made of, and you don't want to abandon them for the grind.

In terms of romantic love, the number 6 can be an indication that new love is on its way to you. As with familial love, you need to turn your gaze away from material possessions in order to find a long-lasting partner. Your heart needs to be open for you to find a connection with another person. If you have your head too much on economic concerns, are constantly in pursuit of money, or focusing too much on objects to collect, you might miss a good partner.

♦ Sit in a comfortable position in a room with minimal decorations or distractions.

As you sit in your clear space, let every
material thing fall away from your consciousness.
You don't need them. Instead, ask yourself what's important
to you in this life. Is it family? Friendships? Community?
Whatever it is, hold that thought in the forefront of your mind.
Then picture the number 6 encompassing it in its center.
Let the characteristics of 6 guide you and put a
magnifying glass on what matters most to you.
Aim for it and let 6 lead you forward.

Angel Number

7

The number 7 is truly a lucky number. When you see 7 pop up in your life, it brings a plethora of good news. The angels are telling you to trust your intuition. Listen to your heart and know that it is leading you where you need to go. At times, it can be difficult to know whether you are doing the right thing, but thankfully 7 is telling you that you are on the correct path and can trust yourself to go even further. You have been in tune with your spiritual side, and it is calibrated to guide you through your journey.

Now that you can trust your intuition, know that the number 7 is a message telling you that you have reached a certain level of awareness and enlightenment. You are now in a position to experience some potentially inexplicable things. You might see more and more signs from the angels that you don't need too much effort to decode. The world around you might look clearer, crisper, and that allows you to truly see your environment as it is. During this time of heightened awareness, you may begin to develop psychic abilities.

If you feel your third eye opening more and more, this could be a sign to explore that aspect of your spiritual being. The number 7 is about spirituality, and that means all facets of it. When the angels send you this number, they are telling you to expand your abilities and discover new parts of yourself you haven't been able to examine before. Nurture your newfound psychic abilities and let them lead you from one level of awareness to another. Let yourself grow and know the angels are telling you that you are on the right path.

With the influx of good news, 7 is also a reminder to celebrate life as it is. You have come very far, and you deserve a little praise and reward. It takes commitment, drive, and discipline to become a fully formed spiritual being, and you have done it. Do not think about what's next or what you have not yet done. Instead, rejoice and relax. This is a time to celebrate, indulge in some self-care, and be fully in tune with your spiritual self. When you see 7, take a moment to acknowledge where you began and where you are now. Be in awe of how far you've come.

- ♦ Sit in a comfortable position.
- ♦ Have a chalice, preferably with a 7 somewhere on it, with a celebratory drink inside.
- ♦ Play happy music.

Meditation

Get comfortable and hold your drink in your hands.
Close your eyes and let the notes of your
music float through the air.
Feel the joy emanating from it.
Next, picture yourself in the presence of God,
surrounded by angels who are so proud of you.
They move about you and tell you that you have done
the work and now you are in a good place.
Take that in, and when you feel the most elated,
take a gulp of your drink.
Savor its taste and know you've earned it.

Angel Number

8

The number 8 represents balance, with one circle above the other. Turned on its side, 8 represents infinity, a never-ending cycle of left and right. Because of this, angel number 8 may represent many things when seen abundantly. One message the angels might be trying to send you is to be grateful for what has come to you so far. Every human alive right now exists because of the infinite choices, discoveries, mishaps, and revelations of those who came before them. There truly is *so* much to be thankful for, more than we could ever fully comprehend.

Use this gratitude all the while you're seeing 8. It is possible to be grateful but also unhappy with one piece of your life. Do not let that unhappiness send you down a road of negativity. Because of the nature of the number 8, it is easy to let one negative thought snowball into another and another. Soon, you'll be stuck in your head only seeing the bad that life has brought you instead of balancing it out with the good. There is room for negative emotions in a person's life. We're all allowed to have them, but do not sit in them for long. Your angels are telling you to stay positive.

If you are currently going through a difficult time and you see 8 appearing, it could be a sign from the angels that these times will end. Everything in the Universe is about balance and cycles. It cannot rain forever, just like it cannot be sunny forever. But that does not mean the bad periods are not useful or even beneficial. According to the energies of 8, the triumphant and disappointing moments are of equal importance and value. Additionally, our thoughts and reactions to these shifts have a way of coming back to us. What you give is what you get. So, when 8 makes itself known in your life, remember that life is always a balancing act.

Sometimes in that act, you are tipping toward success. If 7 is a sign you are on the right path, then 8 is a sign you are close to manifesting your dreams and desires. Also, 8 precedes 9, which means it is the step right before your dreams are actualized. Keep the faith because you are literally almost there.

♦ Sit in a comfortable position.

♦ Have a piece of paper and a consecrated pen.

Meditation

Take your pen and draw an 8 in one motion.
Carefully, make sure each circle is drawn as a perfect circle.
Look at your drawing and use your finger to follow the curves.
This number is powerful and has the capability to teach you so much.
Close your eyes and picture 8 in your mind.
Imagine it glowing with fire, burning bright.
Now tell yourself, "I have infinite potential to handle
infinite scenarios," and know it to be true.
You are much stronger than you think,
especially with the angels on your side.
You can achieve anything as long as you stay balanced.

Angel Number

9

As the last number in the root number set, 9 carries the energy of completion. It symbolizes the end of a journey, a phase in your life, or the fulfillment of your life purpose. When you see the number 9 repeatedly, the angels are trying to tell you that a chapter in your life is about to close, and you may move on to the next adventure. The number 9 represents the "end" of a cycle before returning to 0. Because it is symbolic of the end of a cycle, there is now room for you to view the world in an even more positive light. You have completed a chapter and that means you may enjoy the fruits of your labor. Yet it can also lead you to your next path.

The number 9 is rooted in your life purpose, meaning it may show you another route for you to fulfill it. This can mean letting go of what no longer applies to you. As we move about life, there are coping mechanisms and thought patterns that get us to where we are. But now that 9 has been sent to you, this means you may let these things go in order to move on to the next phase. You can learn to fill your life with positive people and energies so that you may move forward. So, if you see 9 repeatedly, the angels are trying to tell you to take stock of your life and purge all that you do not need anymore.

The number 9 is also the number of love and service to others. In this life, many of us might be in pain or feel lonely and defeated, and this in turn can make us meaner and bitter instead of compassionate and kind. This is not healthy emotionally or spiritually. This number is a message from your angels to use your gifts and talents to help others. This may mean extending a kind word to someone, perhaps paying for someone else's bill, or simply offering some wisdom. Take the time to be kind to those around you because we are all on this planet together and we can all use some grace.

Though you can and should help others, 9 encourages you to also take the help offered to you. With the number 9, your angels are reminding you that it is all right to receive good things from those around you.

♦ Sit in a comfortable position.

♦ Hold nine clear quartz crystals in your hands for purity and new beginnings.

Meditation

Close your eyes and move the crystals about in your hands.
They are a reminder of your physical self,
and they act as conduits for another world.
Now, imagine there is a trodden path behind you.
This represents your previous journey
and what has brought you to this moment.
Before you are three roads, one white for new beginnings,
one pink for love and service,
and one purple for your life purpose.
You must choose one path.
Choose whichever speaks to you the most.
When you have decided, go forward with your whole heart.
The angels are with you.

Angel Number

10

The number 10 is the end and beginning of a cycle of life. Coming in after 9, number 10 is both a number of completion and a number of inception. It takes the energies of 1, which is for fresh starts, and 0, which is for all things Spirit and interconnectedness. When the angels send you the number 10, it means you are entering a new spiritual phase of your life that has been built off the previous phase. You are standing tall on what you have recently accomplished and are using it as a springboard to the next era. Be proud, because in order to reach this phase, you would have had to complete the mission you were meant to.

Now that you have gone through a level of metamorphosis, the number 10 carries with it the energy of planning for the future. It is the intermediary step before starting anew. But this time, you have the knowledge and wisdom to better proceed. Gone are the days of ignorance; now you are a sophisticated spiritual being who knows how to navigate your world. With everything you've learned in mind, you are ready to be even better than you have ever been while striving for a greater future. You have the power you need and the angels as your support.

Because you have learned so much, you have ascended into somewhat of a spiritual leader. You have gone through trials, have overcome them, and now have a whole new perspective. The angels are telling you now that you need to share the skills you've obtained and the wisdom you've found with others. There are so many people who haven't been able to tap into their spiritual sides. Maybe they haven't the heart or the time, or they aren't even aware that there is more to life than what they see. This is where you can come in and share with others so they can grow and benefit as well.

Now that you are here, the angels are telling you that you can speak to your Higher Self. Your Higher Self is the part of you that exists outside of the physical world. Because of this, it does not have a lot of the limitations that you have here on this planet. It is *you*, so it knows you better than you know you. Ask for its wisdom as you carry what you've accomplished into the next stage of your life.

♦ Sit in a comfortable position.

♦ With a skin-safe marker, write a 1 on the back of your left hand and a 0 on the back of your right.

♦ Take five normal breaths and five deep breaths.

Meditation

Close your hands together as if in prayer.
You have combined 1 and 0 to make the spiritual 10.
Keep your hands together and picture yourself on an elevator.
You start on floor 0 and slowly move up to floor 10.
Imagine stepping out of the elevator into a room full of stars.
The Universe is right above you.
The sky is the limit for you and what you can accomplish.
While here, thank God and thank your Higher Self
for being there for you on this pathway.

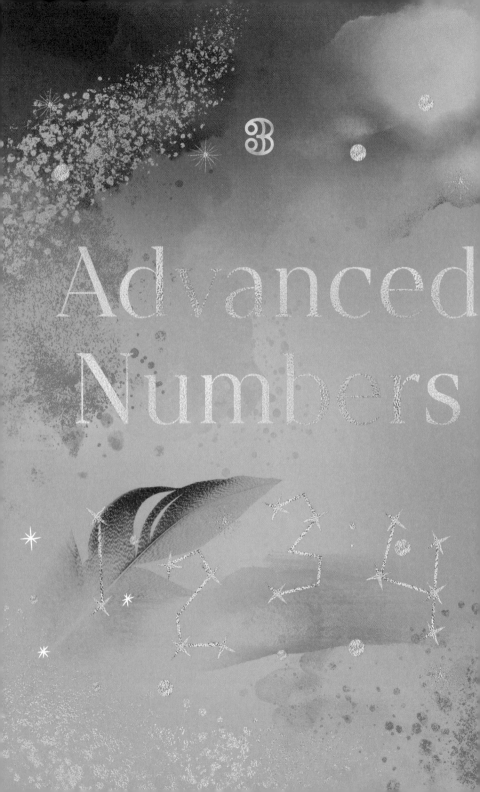

3

Advanced Numbers

NOW THAT WE'VE GONE OVER the root numbers, we can move on to advanced numbers. These numbers contain more developed messages than those of the root numbers. Advanced numbers combine the additions of their digits, pairs of numbers, and the numbers themselves to determine their meaning. The number combination 1234 can translate to $1 + 2 + 3 + 4 = 10$, which can be further reduced to $1 + 0 = 1$. Or it can be read as 12 and 34. Seeing angel numbers like these takes a little more time to decipher, but they can also offer a variety of interpretations.

In this chapter, we will look into the Master Numbers (11, 22, 33), three-digit angel numbers ranging from 1 to 9, and number sequences. Each section builds off the numbers that have come before them to create new meanings. These numbers can be read as their root number multiplied, with 111 meaning 1 times three, or the original meaning of the three-digit number. This book provides a guide

111 5 999 7 1234 33

to each number's message, but feel free to interpret them as the angels guide you. At this stage of angel numbers, your intuition has increased, and you will be able to read and remember the messages much better than you used to at the beginning of your journey. Let it, and the angels, lead you from now on.

Angel Number

11

The number 11 is the beginning of what is called Master Numbers. These numbers carry powerful energies and even more powerful messages, and 11 is known as the teacher number, meaning you have much to learn if you are seeing this number often. If 11 appears, *pay attention* because it means your guardian angels want you to truly hear its message.

The first message might be one of a spiritual awakening. Perhaps you have been distracted by so many aspects of your life, like surviving in this stressful society, maintaining your hobbies, or taking care of your family. These are all important parts of life, but they may also cause you to lose sight of your spiritual self, and that is one of the worst things you can do. If you ignore or push this part of you away, you not only miss out on replenishing your soul, but it will also be more difficult to see or interpret the angel numbers that come your way. With 11, your angels are telling you to ask yourself whether you are on the right path to happiness, prosperity, and growth. Is what you are doing now worth it, or do you find yourself needing more?

Because it is tied to spiritual awakening, 11 is a powerful, hallowed number. It represents faith without reason. Much of numerology and angel numbers is about faith—in the angels, the messages, God, and yourself. Use this confidence, knowing your angels are by your side as you go through this eye-opening time in your life. Look inside yourself and ask whether you have been dutiful or whether doubt has crept into your heart. If so, your angels are trying to tell you to trust your intuition and move in the direction you know is best for you.

When you see 11, know that your angels might be telling you to stay positive and trust your abilities. In order to thrive, you must surround yourself with positive thinking and people. They, along with the angels, will encourage you to be a better version of yourself, and that will help you focus on your purpose. In this life, we are all meant to do *something*, and this number is telling you to set your sights on it and go for it. Have faith in yourself and know that God and the angels have your back. You are in good hands and always will be.

♦ Sit in a comfortable position.

♦ Call upon God to guide you on this meditation.

♦ Place your hands on your heart.

♦ Take two deep breaths for trust and belief.

Meditation

Open your mind's eye to a figure in the room with you.
This being is your guide on this journey.
Reach out for their hand and let them take it.
As you stand with this entity, let their vibrational energy
channel into you, heightening your awareness.
Ask yourself whether you have been faithful to your
journey or have you had some reservations.
Whatever the answer, imagine the being telling you,
"Believe in yourself and your choices."
Ponder this phrase and let it wash over you like rain
until you feel it in your bones.

Angel Number

22

The number 22 is a truly remarkable angel number. It has the energy of both 11, the number of spiritual awakening, and 4, the number of organization and hard work. It is the most powerful of angel numbers because it carries the energy of commanding manifestation. This is exactly why it is a Master Number. People who are drawn to the number 22 are dream builders. What they aspire to may seem impossible to the rest of us, but they believe with all their might and it comes true. When the angels send you 22, be prepared for your goals to manifest quickly. If your life purpose and dreams are in line, then 22 confirms that nothing can stop them from coming true.

Because of its energies, 22 is a number based in logic and reasoning. This might sound counterintuitive, especially when discussing dreams that seem impossible. The truth is, any wish that has ever come true has had to go through a person in order to materialize. This means the dream itself comes from the heavenly plane, but still needs a physical channel to go through in order for it to take form. So, when you see 22, know that the dream is only in the mind until you take the actions necessary to fully realize it.

Though the number 22 carries so much good news, it can also be a sign that you may not be living up to your potential. Do not take this message as one of failure. There are many reasons a person does not meet a certain mark. Perhaps you aren't aware of how powerful you are. Maybe you aren't sure of your life purpose, so you don't aim for it. But if the angels send you 22, they are telling you that you need to wake up to what you are capable of. You are meant to change the world in your own way, so get to it.

It's critical to heed the message of 22 because if you don't, it can have the exact opposite effect on your life. Instead of being organized and focused, you may become careless, overwhelmed, and nervous, or suffer from excessive internal pressure. When you see 22, *listen* to what it has to say. Let it, and the angels, guide you to what you must do next in order to live your life the way you should, the way you're meant to.

- ♦ Sit in a comfortable position.
- ♦ Invite the angels to be there with you.
- ♦ Take two candles of any color and inscribe a 2 on each one.
- ♦ Light the candles.

Gaze into the candles' flames and take note of their numbers.
Imagine the numbers sparking against the candles.
Like any dream, all it takes is a spark to beget a wild, furious fire.
Imagine your life purpose like this, a fire waiting to get started
to completely change the landscape of the world.
Fate is on your side. You know your life purpose,
and nothing will stop it now.

Angel Number

33

The number 33 is the second-most powerful number of the angel numbers because it is the number of love. This encompasses more than just the love of one person for another. It's about a deep, compassionate love for all people that goes beyond one being. This number carries the energy of 11 times three. Remember that 11 is the number of spiritual awareness and 3 is a number of the Ascended Masters urging you to see others through the eyes of God. It is a profoundly spiritual number that exposes the connection between us and the Divine. So, when the angels send you 33, know you are about to get a major change in perspective.

Because 33 is a Master Number, it reflects the attitude of service. The Ascended Masters who have come before us reached enlightenment and actively shared their wisdom with those around them. For you, this can be lending your skills to a worthy cause. It can be sharing your resources with other people, anything that helps others in a tangible way. When you constantly see 33, it's an encouragement to take what you know and what you've created and turn it toward the world. You never truly know how your words or actions will affect those who experience them. Move forward with all your heart and take care knowing the angels and the Ascended Masters are with you.

Being in harmony with the message of 33 means you are feeling love for other people, even the ones you don't know. And when this happens, you are aligned with the spirit of God. Love is heavenly and when you're there, you're close to God. Your relationship with God and the angels is extremely important because it will connect you to yourself and the spiritual plane. Fostering this connection will only ever benefit you. Talk and pray to God and be open to the affection you will receive.

But the most important message of the number 33 is to love yourself. It might sound saccharine, but it's true. When you have love for yourself, that leads to so many other benefits. Self-love gives way to confidence and knowing yourself deeply. This then turns into knowing your goals and desires. The only way you can give to others is when you are fortified with what you need to give yourself. And it's in this way that you can truly help those around you. Cherish the love within and turn it outward.

- ◆ Sit in a comfortable position.
- ◆ Take three deep breaths for God, yourself, and others.
- ◆ Place your hands on your heart.

Meditation

As your hands rest on your heart,
feel the heat radiate from your chest into your hands.
Think the words, "I love myself as God loves me."
Then imagine that warmth spilling from you
to the people in your home, the people in your life,
then the people you're going to meet.
Know in your heart that you will touch lives
more than you will ever know.
Ask God to guide you with this precious life mission.

Angel Number

111

This is one of the most common angel numbers people see. Generally speaking, 1 is everywhere. It's the first number we learn, and the one we will interact with most often because it represents beginnings. Angel number 111 carries similar energies to root number 1 and Master Number 11. When the angels send you 111, they're telling you that you are entering a phase of manifestation. Your goals and wishes can and will come true during this particular point in time. If you have been considering a new life path, this is the perfect time to get started. Make a conscious effort to ponder how you'll be taking the next steps in your life.

Because this is a time of manifestation, you'll be up against the law of attraction. This philosophy says that "like attracts like." Whatever you surround yourself with is what you are going to attract. During this time, focus on positive thoughts and success. Avoid any major negative thoughts. You need to keep your eyes and your mind on the prize. Think about what you want and imagine yourself getting it. Be confident in your next steps and decide that you will get what you want.

If you have been sticking to manifesting your goals, another interpretation of this message is that you are on the right track as a whole. The path you're currently on is the best one for you. When you see this number, especially after doing spiritual work, be content knowing you are doing your best and you're on your way to enlightenment. Stay on the path and do not let any doubt get to you. There are times when we may expect misfortune because of past experiences. We might get the idea that everything is too good to be true and let that get in the way of our current progress. Stay the course.

While carrying the tutelage energy of 11, number 111's message also includes that of fierce self-reliance or being a leader. If you have already done the work, you could be moving into a space of leadership in your community or even in your close circle. You might be coming from a background of organized religion, but now you want to branch out on your own. The message of 111 is that you're gaining independence and you have what it takes to rise up as a leader in your own right.

♦ Sit in a comfortable position.

♦ Hold a piece of tumbled clear quartz for clarity.

Meditation

Hold the quartz in your hands and use it
as a reminder to let go of all other thoughts.
Clear your mind of every distraction.
Now, be very careful and focus only on
what you intend to manifest.
Hold that goal in your mind.
Look at it through all possible angles,
then choose to think about how everything can go right.
Imagine yourself achieving exactly what you want.
Picture it now as if it has already happened.
Keep this up until you see your dream come to life.

Angel Number

222

Similar to angel number 2, number 222 is predominantly about balance in all things. Everything in the world is about balance and the two sides to every situation. Life itself is a struggle to maintain equilibrium. Though 2 is representative of balance, it is also the number of division. Us versus them or, more commonly, us versus ourselves. You may be battling with yourself over your perceived shortcomings, your struggle to do the right thing in any situation, or even the exertion needed to survive in an unfair world. When you battle with yourself, you lose, so when you're fighting from within, listen to 222 and remember that you need to maintain balance so that there is room for growth.

Angel number 222 may appear in your life when the angels see that you are putting too much effort into other things or people that make you unhappy. The nature of life is that we must interact with obstacles to our own happiness—work, strife, rude or inconsiderate people. Of course, we manage as best we can, but there may come a time when you are giving these things too much of your attention and emotional effort. The angels are telling you to slow down and assess what you're giving the most focus to and put some of it back into yourself. If you are not in harmony, nothing else will be.

Other forms of imbalance your angels may notice in your life are impatience and confusion. These qualities tend to come out when we are not in sync with our spiritual selves, or when we are going through difficult periods in our lives. There are seasons when nothing seems to be going right. We may have trouble at work, our personal relationships are suffering, or we simply aren't getting what we want. When you see 222, your angels are telling you to trust whatever is happening to you. It may seem as though you are caught in a spiral of bad fortune but, in fact, everything is happening as it should. Trust the process.

At times, you may feel as though nothing is moving forward and you're stuck in the same position you've been in for weeks or months. Don't worry. Even though it doesn't seem like it, you are progressing. You're always progressing. Never forget that.

♦ Sit in a comfortable position.

♦ Hold an oblong obsidian crystal for balance.

Meditation

Take the obsidian and place it horizontally on one fingertip.
Try your best to keep it balanced on your finger.
There's some difficulty but after a while, you will get it right.
An oblong crystal has two sides, two ends, that must be
kept in check, or the whole crystal will fall.
With practice and care, you can make
the obsidian balance perfectly well.
Stay focused on the important tasks at hand.
Leave no room for negativity and doubt.

Angel Number

333

The number 333 carries the properties of 3, tripled. Number 3 is about creation and creativity. It encourages the person receiving the message to turn to their innovative side and invoke creativity in others. However, 333 encourages us to identify and hone in on our natural abilities. We all have natural talents, even if we don't think so. The trick to finding them is to follow what you enjoy doing most and what others may have told you you're good at. Follow these paths and see what raw potential you have in you. When you find where you excel, nurture that skill, and when you're done, show others for your own spiritual fulfillment. Talent shines best when others can recognize it.

Alternatively, you might be going through a particularly dry season, spiritually speaking. For one reason or another, you might have your head in the proverbial sand, not opening yourself up to the angels or God. Maybe you are extremely busy with your physical life or perhaps you're in a lot of pain emotionally and don't have the capacity to be any more vulnerable than you already are. So, you put your spiritual self on hold. If you are seeing 333 often, it could be the angels trying to get your attention to remind you they exist and so does your soul. You might be straying from the path and the angels might be warning you to get back where you belong.

If this is the case, feel free to call on God and the Ascended Masters for help. They have attained enlightenment and know the trials of being human. If you are drifting further away from your life path, ask them for guidance. There is no reason to struggle alone when you have so many beings willing and able to help you. The Ascended Masters will aid you in return, if you let them.

Keeping your mind solely on spiritual matters can be exhausting. Growth, your life purpose, and the spiritual realm are heavy topics to constantly have on your mind. If you are seeing 333, the angels may be reminding you to have some fun. Don't forget that 3 is a number of joy and enthusiasm. Take time for yourself to enjoy what you can in this life. There's art, nature, thrills, and peacefully quiet nights to relish. Do what you can to find contentment in the physical world.

- ♦ Sit in a comfortable position.
- ♦ Put three fingers in the air from both hands and let them touch, creating a triangular shape.

Meditation

Three is one of the foundational numbers of the Universe.
It's represented in mind, body, and spirit,
and also birth, life, and death.
Use your fingers to bring this point home.
The message of 333 means knowing our talents,
keeping our souls alive, and enjoying life.
Take these three aspects and sit with them now.
You can do all these tasks.
You can be a fulfilled person, rich with life.
Do the best you can and be the best you can be.
That's all you can ask of yourself,
and it's all the angels ask of you.

Angel Number

444

Like the core number 4, angel number 444 is about stability and dedication. Many foundations are made with four points, such as homes, vehicles, appliances, and so on. In order for these things to work, they need to be reliable. We as people also need to be dependable and steadfast to get anything we want done. Though there are periods when we may be loyal and dedicated to our life purpose, we might not see the fruits of our labor. This can be extremely frustrating when it seems like there is no end in sight. When you see 444, the angels are letting you know you should keep going because your hard work is contributing to your future.

Simply listening to angelic messages and doing the work emotionally and mentally to become a better person is enough to be proud of. Becoming in sync with the deeper parts of yourself is no easy feat. It takes time, bravery, and vulnerability to grow into an even better version of yourself with each passing day. Know that not everyone is willing to do the work you have been doing. So, when you have done better for yourself and you see 444, the angels are letting you know to be proud. Yes, they help and guide you, but that advice would mean nothing if you didn't take it seriously and acted on it. Celebrate yourself and sit in the knowledge that *you* did that.

The number 444 is also a reminder to make time for your relationships. No one truly does anything without *some* help. And the relationships in your life support you and lift you up day to day. Remember to nurture those connections, otherwise you might truly be doing it all on your own, and no one wants that. Remind the people closest to you that you care about them and are thankful for their presence in your life.

If you so happen to get caught up in relational drama or stuck in your own head about who knows what, then the number 444 might suggest that you ground yourself. This means ignoring the doubt, anxiety, and unhelpful emotions you might be encountering. Instead, sit in stillness and remember that you can root yourself in the here and now. All we have, as people, is the present moment. Take it and use it to calm you.

♦ Sit in a comfortable position.

♦ If possible, find a square object in your home to hold or gaze at.

♦ Close your eyes and take four deep breaths.

Meditation

After your last breath, sit quietly.
Count four descriptors, like the temperature
of the room or how you feel.
Once you have done so, slowly and deliberately
settle in the present moment.
If your mind drifts to other things, let it,
but come back to the here and now.
You've done what you needed to do,
seen what you needed to, and now
you are here, living, breathing.
Take solace knowing you are on the
right path, and you work tirelessly.
It is enough. You are enough.

Angel Number

555

The number 5 is a big sign of change. It means several alterations are about to happen in your life, potentially all at once. Angel number 555 is no different. When you see this number, prepare for a lot of personal transformations. The number 5 is also about personal freedom and individualism. These are components everyone should have in their lives. Yes, we're part of a collective, but we're also individual human beings with our own matters we face every day. Focusing on ourselves doesn't have to mean we are selfish. It can simply mean we are developing into the person we are meant to be.

With personal change comes letting go of the past and looking toward the future. This can be difficult because we are composed of our past selves and experiences. But when you see 555, the angels are telling you to loosen up and be flexible. It doesn't have to break you and will only make you better. Even so, it's much too easy to cling to what you know in fear of what may come your way. The angels are asking you to believe and trust in your previous choices and what they will bring you now.

With metamorphosis comes personal growth and with growth comes a tapestry of maturity. Our lives are made of stories and experiences we have gone through and overcome. If you're seeing 555 often, the angels might be calling on you to tell your personal story and share it. This could be at church, online, in groups, anywhere. Stories are surprisingly powerful and effective methods for change. Your story is different from another person's even if the chain of events is similar. Take pride in what you've gone through and share it with the knowledge that someone will be positively affected by it.

Seeing 555 often can also be a message of compassion and understanding. We as people struggle and carry that strife with us everywhere we go, despite our best efforts to put it aside. Sometimes this can manifest in a short temper or nasty behavior. We may be too caught up in our own pain that we inadvertently spread it to others. When you encounter this, be kind. Everyone's doing the best they can. Recall a time when someone gave you grace when you were being difficult. Try to see everyone through the eyes of God.

- ♦ Sit in a comfortable position.
- ♦ Fold your hands in prayer and place them against your third eye.
- ♦ Take five deep breaths.

Meditation

After your last exhale, think about the
story of your life and what that has entailed.
Think of your triumphs, your failures,
your happy accidents, and your obstacles.
They have all made up who you are.
They're setting you up for the next moment in your life.
No matter what will come next, you will always
have the history of what came before.
Share this with others and learn from their stories.
Change is natural and so is tenacity.
Live and be you.

Angel Number

666

The number 666 has a bad reputation as being a number of the Devil, one of evil, but that is not what 666 means in numerology or angel numbers. It's simply a message from your angels. If you see this number, do not be afraid. It isn't a bad omen or a curse sent to you. Angels will never send you or cause you any harm. Remember, all their messages are given with love and meant to benefit your life, never to scare you or hurt you. So, until you get used to it, when you see 666, take a deep breath and remind yourself it's all good.

The next step to interpreting 666 is to pay attention when it shows up. What were you just thinking about? Narrow it down to the exact thought because 666 appears as a response to what you're going through. For example, if you are thinking about a project for school or preparing for an interview and you see 666, it's a message telling you that everything will be all right. Six is the number of balance, so 666 carries triple the energy. No matter how out of control everything feels, you will get through it. Trust your abilities and intuition to guide you.

Because 666 carries the energy of equilibrium, it can also be a warning that your life is significantly imbalanced. You might be caught in a never-ending spiral of negativity. One thing after another brings you down and you feel trapped. Or you could be systematically blaming yourself for the state of things you cannot control. You may be telling yourself it's your fault your life is not as you want it to be and that pushes you further into darkness. Angel number 666 says that you need to be balanced. Look at your life as a series of ups and downs. Sometimes there's no conceivable reason everything is falling apart, but you must find the good even in the bad. That is how you achieve peace.

Another form of imbalance is not having respect for yourself. This is an internal battle where you do not give yourself the credit, praise, or recognition you deserve. You can never be balanced if you don't see yourself for the miracle that you are. When the angels send you 666, know that you need to have love for yourself. It all starts within for our lives to improve without.

♦ Sit in a comfortable position, preferably cross-legged.

♦ Place your hands on your knees and hold this position throughout.

Meditation

Close your eyes and take six deep breaths.
With each breath, feel yourself relaxing more into the moment.
Next, picture yourself in a black and white room.
The room is evenly split. Now, see the three 6s,
one on the black side, one on the right,
and one in the middle where the room splits.
In life, there will always be a dark, light, and gray side.
There's no helping it, so we must accept it.
Know that you will never have everything
balanced perfectly, but you must try.
When in doubt, come back to this room
and see the reality of the situation.

Angel Number

777

As we learned earlier, 7 is the number of spirituality. It can be a sign to raise yourself to a certain level. However, 777 is a sign that miracles are on their way to you. These miracles are not determined by how spiritual or well-behaved you have been. Instead, they are simply the natural progression of your journey. These miracles might appear when you're in a dark and troubling phase in your life, or they might stem from the culmination of all your internal, spiritual work. Regardless, they will amaze you and renew your faith in everything you believe in.

The number 777 can also be a sign that you are in sync with the Universe. When broken down, Universe means one (uni) song (verse). So if you are in sync, it's like being in harmony with the greatest and oldest song in existence. This means your angels are also close to you and want to further assist you on your spiritual path. If you're seeing 777, you're in good standing with your angels and with God. Continue what you're already doing and feel your bond with them grow even closer.

At times, we may ignore our inner lives because of what we have to do outwardly. But when you see 777, the angels may be hinting at you to turn inward—not simply to grow more spiritual, but to nurture your inner self. This could mean taking a good look at yourself and getting reacquainted. What is it you like to do? What brings you joy? Who are you without all your titles like worker, parent, or friend? Answering these questions can reconnect you to yourself and this can make you more confident and content with who you are.

Angel number 777 can also be a message telling you to stay curious. Being curious means that you are open to receiving new information, researching, and exploring. Having this attitude means that there's always something to learn, and that will enrich who you are as a person while providing you with the knowledge to better move about your life. Release your inner child and follow your curiosities. If something seems interesting, look into it. If you come to realize you don't know a lot about a certain subject, learn more. The angels are trying to tell you to follow your heart and see what kind of person you become.

♦ Sit in a comfortable position with your palms facing up.

Meditation

Sit in silence and let your mind wander
until it quiets on its own.
Then ask your angels to gather around you
so you can feel their presence.
Close your eyes and wait for them.
They may appear as clusters of light
or have ethereal bodies.
Let them get closer and surround you.
Open your palms and say,
"I accept your help and your love."
Feel them rally with you and
feel their affection for you.
You are loved, you are watched over,
and you are whole.

Angel Number

888

Along with being a number of balance, the core number 8 is a number of abundance, similar to infinity. There are infinite ways you can receive abundance: financially, relationally, spiritually, and more. Whichever form you receive will be specific to you and your life journey. You have been working hard and doing your best, so you will see the rewards for your actions. Seeing 888 means that your treasure is on its way to you. You won't know when it will arrive, but just be patient and continue your work. Good things will come on time.

Let the message of 888 renew your confidence and dreams. When you see this sequence, the angels may be telling you to reach even higher than you've ever dreamed. There are times when we may doubt the possibility that our desires can come to fruition. We may think they are too lofty or unreasonable to achieve. With 888, your angels are saying to dream even bigger. Do not shy away from what you really want. Your blessings are already coming to you. Take them and aspire for more. It's in your power. It's your right.

Because you have worked to attain your blessings, you may think you can control when these things come to you. Manifestation is very real, but it isn't something we can control. Instead, it's something that comes to us as a combination of our actions and heavenly timing. The number 888 holds the energy of strong authority and strong will, meaning that when we see this number, we may get overzealous and want to be completely in charge. Life does not work this way, especially with God and the angels. It is perfectly all right to be strong-willed, but remember you are one piece of the Universe, so do your part and know the rest is out of your hands.

When you try to remain in control, you may get the idea that you really can conduct everything around you—your life, your relationships, or your coworkers, for example. When the angels send you 888, know this is a reminder to let go and enjoy your life as it is. Don't continuously try to steer it. Let it happen and revel in your blessings. When you let go of control, you can begin to relax and trust in God.

♦ Sit in a comfortable position.

♦ Relax your jaw, forehead, shoulders, and hands.

Meditation

Close your eyes and let go of any tension in the body.
Open your hands as if you are reaching up to receive a gift.
Take a deep breath and say aloud, "God and the angels,
I humbly accept my blessings with the knowledge that more
will come to me. I'm grateful for them, but I will also aim for
higher goals. I will control my actions and let God do the rest."
Take in what you have just said and let the words
wash over you. You are blessed.

Angel Number

999

Similar to root number 9, the number 999 is the end of the three-digit sequence. And like 9, it represents the end of a cycle of life and harks to the origin of a new one. We might give endings a sad connotation, but in reality, an end can be the best thing that has ever happened to someone. It's the chance to move forward, away from the past, and into a glittering, shining future. When you see 999, the angels are telling you to let go of the old and embrace the new. This can be nerve-racking because the new is the unknown, but sometimes fear is a sign that you are emerging from your comfort zone into a state of metamorphosis.

As you are approaching a new chapter, use this time to take stock of past behaviors and thought patterns. Do you keep a journal? If so, consult it and see where you started in this current cycle. Ask yourself what you did in the beginning. How did you handle yourself during this time? What could you have done better? And where did you shine? Looking through your past can be a road map to your future. Here you can see from a distance how your life has played out and what you can use to move to the next stage. And most importantly, be proud of what you've been through and how much you've grown.

As you take stock of your actions, you can see what you went through when you weren't sure what was going on in your life. You are now able to see how scared you may have been and what you needed in those moments. You can see yourself as human and this knowledge can help you empathize with others. Often God and the angels tell us to help those around us. One way to do this is to be gentle and understanding, even when we don't want to be. Everyone can benefit from compassion.

Trust in yourself and the abilities you were born with as well as the abilities you learned while on your life's path. You are a wonder just by being you, and you have a lot to offer the world whether you think so or not. When you see 999, this is an encouragement from the angels, but also a reminder that you should have faith in yourself. You've done the work, you've learned a lot, and you have the power to help others. Your voice and your experiences are important. Never think you are any less than this.

♦ Sit in a comfortable position.

♦ Hold an hourglass or simply imagine one.

Take note of the hourglass.
In it is enough sand to last exactly one hour.
There is a clear beginning and end to its life cycle.
No matter how one tries, you cannot dump all the sand
into one chamber at once. It takes time.
There is a clear beginning that, once started, needs
to be completed before the next cycle begins.
Our lives are like hourglasses. They move slowly
and quickly all at once and no matter how many
times we go through a cycle, the sand never falls
exactly the same way each time.
We are constantly ending and
constantly beginning anew.

Angel Number

1010

Here we are again at the end of another cycle, but similar to 10, this is just the beginning. The angel number 1010 carries the many energies of 1, 0, and 10. Like 10, number 1010 is a spiritual number that references new beginnings and spiritual awakenings. You might see 1010 when you are in a transitional period, closing out an old phase of growth into a new one. The period after 999 and into 1010 is when you may feel yourself turning into a more mature person. Or you may feel like you have reached a spiritual goal you've set for yourself and the effects are taking root inside you. Whatever you feel, take it all in.

Seeing 1010 might also be a sign that you are on the verge of expanding your spiritual consciousness. This results in you becoming more spiritually aware. This awareness can look like you seeing angel numbers much more often, or you can interpret the messages, even the more complex numbers, at first glance. Or you may feel your psychic abilities come into play and that changes how you view the world and your own needs within it. Your third eye expands and sees more than it ever has. In this stage of being, you can also commune with your Higher Self much more often. You might find that its messages aren't as cryptic as they once were. You are on the verge of greatness.

Another message of 1010 is that you are surrounded by love and light. Not only are the angels watching you, but your ancestors are too. They could be loved ones in your immediate family who have passed or even great-grandparents. Whoever they are, they are rooting for you. Seeing 1010 is a reminder that you are never truly embarking on any journey alone. You are constantly loved and being watched over, so don't be afraid to call on your guardians for love and support. That's what they are there for.

There may be times when you are experiencing doubt or confusion about what is going on with you. Maybe your abilities are advancing faster than you can keep up with or you aren't sure whether what you're experiencing is real. When the angels send you 1010, they are telling you to have faith in yourself and to reject doubt. You are very capable, despite what you may think. Charge ahead with confidence and never second-guess yourself.

♦ Sit in a comfortable position.

♦ Hold a photo of yourself in a pivotal moment in your life or anything that represents that moment.

Meditation

Take a look at the photo in your hands.
Who were you in this stage of your life?
What was going on during this time?
What were your challenges and what were your victories?
Right now, you have insight that you didn't have back then.
The current you knows that you matured into the person
you are now because of the person you were then.
Take this perspective and apply it right now.
You are on the verge of something life changing.
Lean into it and don't be afraid.
The angels are telling you it will be all right.

Angel Number

1111

Number 1111 is a magical sequence because it combines the energies of 1 times four, 11 times two, and the combined power of the number 4. This means it's a highly spiritual number, predominantly of manifestation and goal keeping. One explanation of 1111 is that it's a wake-up call, reminding the person who receives it that they are a spiritual being first and a physical being second. So instead of putting all your attention on the material plane, shift your gaze back to your soul and spiritual well-being. This ensures you are taking care of yourself as you are meant to.

Nurturing your soul also means getting your priorities in order. Because 1111 represents a time of manifestation, you should not waste time honing in on anything that doesn't truly matter to you. Instead, pay attention to what enriches you, what feeds you, and what you want to achieve while on this earth. What are your aspirations? What makes you feel like you were born to do it? Prioritize those things in your life because they will be what will ultimately fulfill you and make your life purpose a reality. Get this in order so you will manifest effectively.

When you have your list sorted out, it's time to make a petition. It's a common practice to make a wish when you see 11:11 on the clock. This comes from the idea that 1111 is the number of quick manifestation, similar to 11. So, when you see 1111, make your wish known and God will provide it to you. Keep that wish in mind every time you see 1111 because your thoughts are what will cause your dreams to go into effect. Then use the number 4 to apply practical methods to make your dreams come true.

After this, just believe. When you see the number 1111, the angels are telling you to have unrestricted faith. It's a time to temporarily put logic, doubt, and rationale aside and focus on the possibilities. Of course, working with the angels isn't just about lofty goals and wishes, but there are moments when we must let go of what we think is possible and just believe. When we focus too much on "I can't" or "there's no way," we inhibit ourselves and are not freely expressing what we want out of this life. Our purest desires arise when we release the restraints of logic and just focus on what we want to achieve.

♦ Sit in a comfortable position.

♦ Hold a lucky charm in your hand.

Take a moment to sit with your thoughts.
Don't judge them, just let them come through.
Now shift your attention to the lucky charm in your hand.
People wear lucky charms because they want
the Universe to move in their favor.
Ask yourself what you want God to provide for you.
What are your dreams that you want to manifest?
What luck do you hope comes your way?
Focus on this and this alone.
You're in a time of quick manifestation,
so keep your mind free of distractions.
Be clear on what you want and say it out loud
for God and the angels to hear.

Angel Number

2222

This number is constructed off the backs of 2, 22, and 222, meaning it carries similar energies of power, building, relationships, and peace and serenity. Number 2222 is a combination and an echo of the numbers that came before it. When you see 2222, your angels are telling you to be strong-willed. Do not let people run all over you. Do not let them stomp on you and make you feel less than. Stand strong in yourself and who you are. You're a powerful spiritual being who knows yourself. You never need to put yourself down or let others do the same. Move about your life in this way and you will find that nothing can stop you.

The number 2222 is twice the number 22, which is the number of a Master Builder. This means you should think hard about your decisions before you make them. Every action, whether big or small, contributes to an outcome.

When building anything, you have to make sure you make the right moves each step of the way so that whatever it is you do build will be solid and well-made. The energy 2222 carries is too precious to be spent making rash or half-thought-out decisions. Watch your step and think before you move. Your future may depend on it.

When you see 2222, the angels may be sending you a reminder to nurture your current relationships, especially those in the beginning stages. Number 2 is about relationships and so is 2222. It combines the energies of trust, love, compassion, and kindness. Give these qualities to all your personal relationships and some of them to your professional relationships as well. We are social beings who need those around us to uplift us. The angels are challenging you not to forget that.

Angel number 2222 is also a number of peace and serenity. When you see this number, the angels are telling you to let go of whatever is negatively influencing you and choose to find peace for yourself. Because of the magical vibrations of 2222, we may want to go, go, go to move further along our life's path. But 2222 is also telling us to be serene, because otherwise we are frantic, impatient, and more likely to stop our journey altogether. Especially with all the work you are doing, you need peace in order to recharge. You deserve it.

♦ Sit in a comfortable position.

♦ Draw 2222 on a piece of paper.

Meditation

Gaze upon 2222. Take one pointer finger and
place it on the first 2. Imagine the energy of a strong
character going from the 2 into you. You are
a strong person and you'll let nothing stop you.
Move to the next 2 and do the same. Pull the energy
of construction and use it to fuel your future decisions.
Put your finger on the third 2. Think of your
current relationships and how you can deepen
your connections. Lastly, move to the final 2 and
feel a calm wash over you. Stay in the present
moment and don't think of anything else.
This will propel you forward when the time is right.

Angel Number

3456

The number 3456 is a special number sequence because it doesn't often show up in our lives, so when it does, it's important to pay attention. Because this is a sequential number, 3456 needs to be decoded number by number. Number 3 is about creativity and faith. This can translate to a belief in yourself and belief in God. Creativity comes from the spiritual realm and runs into the material realm through you. It's a message to create with your natural talents and abilities. The way 3456 is structured makes its message one of steps, and 3 is the first one.

The second number in the sequence is 4, which carries the energies of hard work and implementing the steps needed to make your goals come true. In combination with the number 3, this could be a message telling you to explore your creative side in order to manifest your goals, but now you have to apply some practical action to get things off the ground. It's about dedication to your craft and your life purpose. It's important to keep yourself on track and focus on your dreams.

The number 5 is about spiritual changes in your life. Because this number comes after 4, it is a sign that after putting in the work for your spiritual path, you will start to see results. It can also mean you can prune some of the nonessentials from your life to make room for the new spiritual growth. Maybe you made decisions in the 4 stage, and you don't want to repeat them. The 5 in 3456 is telling you to trim down what isn't serving you anymore in order to move forward with what does.

Last, the number 6 is about balance and connections. When you get to this stage in the number sequence, you are being called to remain in harmony. At this point, you will have experienced some major shifts in your life as your plans come to fruition. It's imperative to stick to the path you are on because, clearly, it's working! Don't let anyone who may be envious of your success or spiritual progression get to you. Stay true to your vision and your life purpose. Through them, you will grow closer to the angels and to God. In that, you will find fulfillment and peace.

♦ Sit in a comfortable position.

♦ Write down your most pressing dream or goal you want to manifest.

Meditation

Look at your goal and say this aloud:
"I know my dream will come true because the angels
and God have opened the doors for me.
I am more than capable and more than willing
to put in the work to manifest my goals.
The Divine sees this happening for me,
and I see it happening for myself."
Focus all your thoughts on your goal
as if you are giving the words life.
Concentrate on this and feel your vibrations rise.
You have been blessed with the vision
and you will receive it.

Conclusion

You've made it! You have learned how to receive communications from the angels, you can read their messages, and you know how to make changes in your life for the better. You may be at the end of the book, but that does not mean you are at the end of your spiritual journey. The more you learn, memorize, and understand angel numbers, the more you will be able to intuit even more number combinations. There are myriad angel number sequences that exist and that others have expanded upon. Similar to life, there are so many possibilities and different messages you can receive from God.

From this point onward, keep a diary of all the numbers you see. Keep track of when you see them, what you were thinking, what you were feeling, and what your first impression was. This will paint a clearer picture of where you began, where you are now, and potentially where you're going. Once you have a road map, you will be more prepared to share your story with others and guide those following a similar life path as you. You'll grow a deeper understanding of yourself and what you have to offer the world.

Take this prayer with you for good wishes and a brilliant, fulfilling future.

Meditation

May the angels be with you always.
May they protect you, warn you, love you,
and keep you within the confines of your destiny.
May God watch over you and send you exactly
what you need to flourish on this new path.
You are worthy. You are chosen. You are sublime.
You have what it takes to be powerful and influential.
Never forget where you come from
or what you are made of.
Go forth.

SO MOTE IT BE.

Meditation Index

2. Root Numbers

3. Advanced Numbers

First published in 2023 by Wellfleet Press, an imprint of The Quarto Group,
142 West 36th Street, 4th Floor, New York, NY 10018, USA
T (212) 779-4972 F (212) 779-6058 www.Quarto.com

Wellfleet titles are also available at discount for retail, wholesale, promotional,
and bulk purchase. For details, contact the Special Sales Manager by email at
specialsales@quarto.com or by mail at The Quarto Group, Attn: Special Sales
Manager, 100 Cummings Center Suite 265D, Beverly, MA 01915 USA.

10 9 8 7 6 5 4 3 2 1

ISBN: 978-1-57715-393-1

Library of Congress Control Number: 2023931593

Publisher: Rage Kindelsperger
Creative Director: Laura Drew
Managing Editor: Cara Donaldson
Editor: Sara Bonacum
Cover and Interior Design: Evelin Kasikov
Text: Johanie M. Cools

Printed in China

Continue your spellcraft with these additional companions:

978-1-57715-390-0   978-1-57715-391-7   978-1-57715-388-7

978-1-57715-389-4   978-1-57715-392-4